Desperanto

With thanks &
best wishes,
Jayne !

Mike Wil

Desperanto

Poems by Mike Wilson

STACK
BOOKS

Published 2009 by
Smokestack Books
PO Box 408, Middlesbrough TS5 6WA
e-mail : info@smokestack-books.co.uk
www.smokestack-books.co.uk

Desperanto
Mike Wilson
Front cover photograph: Soviet troops take the Reichstag Building,
Berlin in 1945 (Yevgeni Khaldei/Hulton Archive/Getty Images)
artwork by Fox Graphics, Derby
Author photograph by S. J. Closs

Printed by
EPW Print & Design Ltd

ISBN 978-0-9554028-7-6
Smokestack Books gratefully
acknowledges the support of
Middlesbrough Borough Council
and Arts Council North East

Smokestack Books is
represented by Inpress Ltd
www.inpressbooks.co.uk

Contents

The More or Less Deceived

We mark the milestones, all the peaks and troughs
of marriages, our friendships and affairs,
with gifts of Ferlinghettis and McGoughs,
anthologies of Betjemans and Clares.
The old Romantics!
                    Meanwhile, on the shelves
of former lovers, husbands, confidantes,
thin-spined reminders of our former selves
reproach us, like abandoned maiden aunts…

These Larkins all were Luke's. From different lovers:
High Windows came from Sarah, and Marie
was *Whitsun Weddings*… On the inside covers
each made their dedication (poetry
more poignant than the polished works that follow!),
inscriptions of such hope and reassurance!

But *Forever* and *For Always* now sound hollow,
embarrassing almost beyond endurance…

Marie now keeps the books that once were Luke's,
and Luke survives a former love's rebukes…

And Poetry survives on slender sales
which celebrate a Love that never fails!

Desperanto

Sad poetry. It's written everywhere,
by broken hearts in search of self-expression:
the universal language of despair.

She writes of anguish (and it's hard to bear).
She chisels, from the floes of her depression,
sad poetry. It's written everywhere.

He tries (in vain) to emulate John Clare,
to forge a bridge between his self-obsession and
the universal language of despair.

But he's not self-aware, not debonair,
he lacks the savoir-faire, the self-possession…
Sad poet, try! It's written, everywhere,

that anyone who's sad, and solitaire,
should curse in verse, as if their flair could freshen
the universal language of despair.

And round they go – mad fingers twirling hair
(which tends to give a negative impression:
sad!). Poetry? It's written. Everywhere,
the universal language of despair.

Long Distance

I   Edinburgh Festival, Calton Hill

We're up on Spyglass Hill to see the show –
the spot-lit tower a telescope upright.
As Handel trills from someone's radio
we watch the fireworks inflame the night.

We're both at such a distance, sound is slow –
you hear these things long after they ignite.

Then somebody lights up, and drops the match,
the hill takes flame, an accidental blaze
which snatches at the sky. A red heat-haze
grows quickly, and we move away. It dies
in time, the danger dies. It leaves a scorch-
mark scar, still smouldering, a blackened patch.

Or –
        maybe someone *meant* to light that torch,
a beacon to be seen by far-aways,
competing with the fireworks in the skies…

Meanwhile, a calmer firework, cream and full,
is flirting with the clouds; all I remember's
the same warm moon I watched in Istanbul
a month ago.
                I breathe onto the embers.

II

… back to the flats of single men, I guess.

What fascinates me most is not the fact,
or questions of morality; but more
the little daily details of the act,
the dirty linen strewn on someone's floor.

Do you think it made her love her husband less?
Or more? Stuff that! What I would rather know:
What words d'you find to say? Or: where d'you go? …

Just how do we decide to take a lover?
In terms of what commitment? Is it love?
(Committing things, you later on discover,
is what solicitors accuse you of…)

I drive her to the airport, and we're sitting
for a final hour, before she has to go.
Then, just when I want to say what *I'm* committing,
she has to phone her husband from Heathrow.

III

Today I put your nightdress in a drawer.

I found it in the bed the day you flew
to Turkey. Crumpled, empty and forlorn,
I hung it on the hook behind the door.

So, sometimes in the dark before the dawn,
or, getting dressed some mornings, missing you,
I'd stand and hold the fabric that you'd worn
then taken off, to be more close to me.

It didn't really, somehow, seem to be
quite you: the frills and ribbons and pink braid.
But the scent you left behind was. All your own.
It smelt of us, the sex, the love we made.
I thought that you were captured there forever,
I thought that I could conjure you whenever…

But scents, like memories, are never known
to last for long. They fade. In time, they fade.

So now I've washed your nightie, ironed it flat
and tidied it into a chest of drawers.

You take the things you can't afford to lose
and put them into storage. And that's that.

And there they wait, mementoes, metaphors:
red panties, or your high-heeled, black suede shoes.

IV

He brings a few belongings round of yours.
You find another temporary home
in someone else's house; and I make room
for your posters and another chest of drawers,
an ironing board, a set of folding chairs…
The wardrobe comes apart, and this is good –
it means that we can take it up the stairs
in pieces, without damage to the wood.

But later, on my knees, the thought occurs
(a screwdriver, his little bag of screws
to hand): he took apart these things of hers
an hour ago. How none of us can choose
what is dismantled, or what is rebuilt.
He passes on his memories, and I
just reassemble them. Regrets and guilt
are smothered in the smiles of our goodbye.

The pictures that he hung I hang in turn:
proud Carmen in the arms of Don José.
(We might relate to that infatué!)
But I'm more struck by this ironic twist:
The film poster I keep for your return,
emblazoned with the words: NOT TO BE MISSED!

V

I left them there in one another's arms.
The meal, the drinking done, and she was flinging
herself on him, as if the hurts and harms

of these two years had never really been.
I couldn't bear to watch this brave doomed scene.
I left them there in one another's arms.

When I got home the telephone was ringing.
Delayed reaction strikes again. As if
she realised, in time, this savage clinging
grows meaningless. Your arms ache. Whereupon
she looks – too late – for someone, who'd just gone.
When I got home the telephone was ringing.

The longing hits you later, keen as grief.
The pattern was established with that call:
disjointed conversations, frail belief
in something that was barely there at all
before we stretched and tortured it. Delayed,
sporadic, overlapping letters made
a mockery of contact. Love and all
the longing hit you later, keen as grief.

And now we keep in touch by telephone.
Long distance. And I cannot tell if she
returns to someone's arms, or sits alone
after my late-night calls. Or it may be
we are cut off, call back. The lines get worse.
My own voice overriding hers,
I hear the brave doomed things I say, as we
just try to keep in touch by telephone.

VI

The little things: the brisk, dismissive way
she says, when asked – how are you? – I'm okay…

The little things: not drinking much,
not drunk like me, she looks away, or moves
her foot away, distracted, if I touch
her.

      Slow, confiding smiles on flat-mates' faces.
Impenetrable.
                  All these conversations
in sparse apartments, filled with empty spaces.
(We've happened here from half a dozen nations
to say we hope the weather soon improves…)

The common-place: the lying in her bed
and talking, Larkin-like, beneath that sky;
the things we musn't say, or leave unsaid…

The tears when she was trying not to cry…

The slipping into Turkish on the phone
to Ibrahim…
                 The sleepless nights we share;
(it's getting easier to sleep alone,
or harder getting used to someone there…)

Applauding as we leave the fluttering air
and land in London, I'm still in that bar
in Istanbul. I nudge towards her chair.
Too far away, I quip. (Hah-bloody-hah.)

Airport to airport. We meet, we say goodbye
with mis-timed kisses, platitudes, these fumbling
farewells.
              I left my glass of Turkish çay
undrunk and spilt.
                     The cube of sugar.
                            Crumbling.

Poor Chap, He Always Loved Larkin (and now he's dead)

I lay the Larkin down, and think about
his quiet life. Alone, he had the time
and space to watch a sullen, sour doubt
take hold of him – and craft it into rhyme.

I thought – he had no live-in lover, wife
or family, and seemingly few friends;
this gave him time to live the poet's life.
Was loneliness the means towards the ends?

To have no son, or wife or house or land,
to live without dilutions, in-laws, crappy
conversations which waste their time and ours…
This freed him from the old fools and the bland
and barren days. He chose to spend those hours
on poetry's compulsion.

                                          (Was he happy?)

I'm pillow-propped in bed. My lover dozes.
She's kitten-curled around me, on my shoulder,
the warmth of last night's loving in our noses,
the Larkin, on my chest remoter, colder.

That book weighs heavy on me – heart and mind:
how can I hope to be this poem's shaper
when, passion-spent and sprawling, intertwined,
I'm snatching time to scrawl these scraps of paper?

I lay the Larkin down, and I decide:
You make the most of what you haven't got.
Dispassionate, he analysed his loss,
his otherness embraced and undenied.
He lacked the glare of love's much-mentioned gloss,
and I'll always lack his brilliance.

                                          (So what?)

Dee

I must get round to pouring down the sink
the gift you brought, for me – or us – to drink.
A weekend break in Scotland and you came
back with a whisky labelled with your name.

We blew so hot, so cool that year before,
fire-water was a perfect metaphor:
love-doubt, love-dread and, lastly, love-despair
(those heady fumes evaporate in air).

I can't quite bear to face (and nor can you)
the damage we put one another through
two years ago. The taste of ashes, salt,
cannot be washed away by bitter malt.

And though I can't quite bring myself to taste
your gift, I can't quite watch it put to waste:
to drink would be a meagre celebration,
to throw away would be a lame admission

of failure. I prevaricate. I waver.
(Perhaps it will be on my shelf for ever…)
For the present bears your name; will always be
a miniature of finest River Dee.

Tattoo

At rest now,
passion a passing thing,
a thousand chasms past.

And hands that once clutched, clawed,
flung her aside, clung her back to him -
now sleep in his lap like kittens.

She scratched herself into his skin,
her love hungry as an empty needle,
her love sharp as a shard of glass.

Now,
the years have lost her.
Her face has faded, ink on parchment.

He has forgotten the shudder of her name,
the susurrus-thrill of teeth on lips:

Viv.

'It's Latin,' she'd beam,
'for life.'

He has forgotten those eyes,
wide as open veins,
and the day she gripped his hand 'til it bled.

'For ever,' she'd said.
'I'll be here for life.'

A Pond-skater

In his first relationship,
he was irritated by her hair in his face.
He swung the blades of his hands,
and swept it away.

In his next relationship,
it was the toothpaste tube.
She never seemed to squeeze it
in quite the right place.
He withdrew, hating her,
hated himself, and withdrew.

In his next relationship.
it was the way she pronounced *Nic – ara – hwa.*

The next had never heard of Nicaragua.
He taught her all he knew,
including the correct pronunciation.

Next was clingy.
He withdrew.

The next hooked her ankles behind his,
clung to his buttocks,
bellowed with abandon.
He tried to get used to
the way she talked in cinema queues.

The next one – after a while – never spoke.

Next had a better job than him.

Next had no job.
When she left,
she scratched an angry sketch of him:
a pond-skater,
its feet gentle dents on some immeasurable surface.

For now,
he sleeps alone, wakes early, favours jogging.

In his next relationship, he vows,
he'll sink, and settle,
develop a taste for depths
and sediment.

He'll coax her hair across his face in the mornings
'til it tickles.

Cut Off

how

after the shriek of tears

and the gut-wrenching

after you try to sever the cord of one life

so that another may be born

and fail

you return to the day-to-day

the kitchen conversations

and you hear a voice like your voice

asking:

did you manage to find those scissors,

after all?

The C-Word

His girlfriend's given him the E:
he couldn't do the C-word.
And now the situation is
a total effing B-word.

There's more to it than juggling
those two four-letter L-words.
And so the situation is
heading effing hell-wards.

His brain is working overtime
to keep his heart from grieving,
but thinking thoughts is not enough
to stop her effing leaving.
And a heart is not a hiding place:
it should be worn on sleeving.

Poor B! He'll never understand,
no hope of him conceiving:

Commitment is a leap of faith
and C-ing is believing.

Sleeping Next Door

My partner can't sleep, and she's ready to weep
with despair at her gathering fatigue.
She's tried yoga, and praying, and Ipodly-playing
piano concertos by Grieg.
Counting sheep has been tried, several blindfolds applied,
she's been talking to friends on the phone,
and she's tried marijuana, sleep-tea from Botswana,
hot cocoa, my best Côtes du Rhône…
She's been chanting, and reading, and nocturnal-feeding,
deep-breathing curled up on the floor,
then she tried taking fluorine, and drinking her urine…
She even tried Radio 4.

So she's in the spare room in a gloom-shaded doom
that is near suicidal in tone.
But I have to admit (being a self-centred git)
I'm quite glad that she's left me alone:
On my own in the bed, I've got more room to spread –
I can lie like a star-fish, and read
mucky books, pick my feet, blow my nose on the sheet,
spill the beans till my testicles bleed;
and when she's like this, it's just taking the piss
to expect her to 'make like the whore';
what she needs is massage, not knob-camouflage…
just as well that she's sleeping next door.

Her frustration and fury won't be judge and jury.
I won't feel like Hitler or Stalin
if I start my repose, mumble, dribble and doze
in a different room from my darlin'.
And her wild frenzied cries, inconsolable sighs
and her whispers: 'can't take any more!'
won't filter to me as I sink though the sea…
so I'm glad that she's sleeping next door.
With an internal cheer I eventually hear
that my partner has started to snore.
And there's no sense of shame as I think, without blame:
I'm so glad that she's sleeping

next door.

Fresh Fields

The builders of these terraces might turn
in their grassed-over graves if they should see
what's happened to the neighbourhood they built
a century ago. Perhaps they felt
they made a working-class community
(though now I guess you'd struggle to discern

the working class round here). These houses, planned
for workers from the local factories,
as like as not house the un-working class,
the debris of the Dole Age, now. Alas,
despite the prosperous years that victories
in two world wars (you might think) should have earned,

the people around here are not much richer.
The lace-mill at the bottom of our street,
converted into 'bijoux flats' and 'mewses',
stands empty. It distorts the place, confuses;
the thinking (like the building)'s incomplete.
What happened to the over-locker, stitcher,

the lace-mill labourer, factory hand? And who
replaced the fitter and the artisan
in these thin streets, these narrow-planted houses?
The laid-off labourer; pensioners, their spouses;
poor families from Poland, Pakistan,
Jamaica; all those people in the queue

on pension day and Giro day outside
the sub-post office that sells string, fruit-gums
and dusty birthday cards, as well as doling
out benefits to those beyond consoling;
the double-buggies pushed by single mums
(like post-war widows re-personified).

But what might turn those builders in the grave
(assuming they're in graves, and didn't die
in tawdry wars; and in some far fresh field
there isn't some dead working man's congealed
or bleach-boned grinning skull staring at sky
beneath a neatly-planted row of brave

white crosses in their terraces) is this:
the way the Left have colonised the place.
And not the old traditional Labour voter,
a brave New Left, who couldn't be remoter.
They give Karl Marx a modern, 'nineties' face
- with pony-tail and earring. (You may miss

the irony in this joke – I include
myself: I bought the Bee-Gee beard-trimmer,
the Dr Martens, Marx and Spencer's clothes…)
These are the types that Thatcher no doubt loathes;
and if they're keeping 'leaner, fitter' (slimmer),
they put it down to wholesome veggie food.

We're talking here the 'New Man' and his 'mate'
(these days it's 'partner', or 'co-habitee').
They're the Sainsbury Socialists. They grow wealthy
on guilt-trip politics, mingled with a healthy
scepticism, laced with irony.
They're cynical of what made Britain 'Great',

for instance, or what drags us into wars…
Then there's the Hard Left dogmatists, the band
who keep their Marx in paperback in pockets
in their shabby anti-fashion Oxfam jackets,
who really read *Das Kapital*, and stand
in snow for hours, selling papers for the cause…

Then there's the rest, the disaffected Left:
the Anarchist collective; Asian gays
who pose in perfect clothes and lean on cars
as if they owned them; people with guitars
who can't afford the cases; drunk roués
who'll tell you who wrote 'Property is Theft';

the nostril-punctured punkette, safety-pin
between her eyes; pale Vegan wraiths;
rad.-fem. fatales with (female) dogs in tow...
And renting houses in the self-same row
a dozen different families and faiths,
a different shade to every different skin.

They came to pastures new, to Fresher Fields,
from colonies and (so-called) Third World nations.
They fled from famines, genocides and wars.
In other words, they're symptoms, not the cause.
They're not the architects of their migrations,
they just got pushed. They're squandered pawns, the shields

of kings and bishops. You hear power-brokers,
whenever the economy's beset
and inner-city riots get a mention,
ascribe hostilities to racial tension.
And how the fuck are we supposed to get
that fatuous cliché clearly into focus?

The Ayatollah Khomeini once said
that every nation needs someone to hate:
Americans; the Jews; the Blacks; the Scots;
superior 'haves', despising poor 'have-nots'...
The Ayatollah's concept, the Great Satan,
means everyone has someone to behead.

You'll doubt me, but Fresh Fields is not like this:
it's peaceful here. There may be confrontation
and shouting matches, neighbours get annoyed...
But conflict's mainly something you avoid.
When *they* have wars, *we* have a demonstration
against hypocrisy and avarice.

In '91, the war against Iraq,
was rich in tender irony for me.
For one: amid the pro- and anti- spielers,
a few (non-partisan) smart weapons dealers
lit the blue paper, then immediately
retired to safety for the first attack.

They'd sold both sides the means towards our end.
A stash of cash (or nationalistic pride)
will cushion any blow in fireworks-fights.
Another irony: how human rights
will always be invoked by any side
with a hundred precious oil-fields to defend.

It's January 1991.
The brink of war is on the Saudi border.
The world is poised to overpower Saddam.
It's Christianity against Islam,
technology against the feudal order,
or righteousness against the Evil One,

depending on your viewpoint. In our street
it's peaceable enough. Despite the tension
there's (pre-war) calm, we exercise discretion.
No xenophobic action or aggression,
no incident requiring intervention,
no anti-Muslim insult or graffiti,

no British flags unfurled in White defiance…
No incident at all – unless you can
include my neighbour Mushtaq, who one night
set his alarm for an hour before daylight
(although he must have known that Ramadan
was months away). This hideous appliance,

designed to make the dead wake in their tombs,
has no effect on Mushtaq. He's far gone
(as if he'd drunk a half-a-pint of brandy!)
as an electronic *Yankee Doodle Dandy*
in pitiless repetition twitters on.
The party walls are thin: in next-door rooms

his neighbours groan and stir, and start to cough
- then batter walls and bellow at the man
out-cold next door: A fire alarm you want!
You work too hard. (That bloody restaurant!)
You're not a Yankee, you're from Pakistan!
For God's sake, wake up! Turn the bastard off!

Another incident: the night the war
began, Mudassar, Mushtaq's little son,
stuck both hands in a blender, and his third
and little fingers were cut off. I heard
a frightened nurse: 'they've started, everyone…'
at midnight in an A&E corridor…

On Bonfire Night, November the same year,
we gathered on the Forest for a fire
(a souvenir of safer conflagrations),
to celebrate the rescue of the Nation's
Democracy from desperate men's desire
to make the House of Commons disappear.

(And though today we may have sympathies
with Catesby and the rest, we acquiesce
when feckless thatchers, majors, men of straw,
consign a fellow scarecrow to the raw
oblivion of flame. Forgetfulness,
not memory's preserved when effigies

are raised.) It felt like everyone was there,
all huddled in, at one another's shoulder
for warmth and for community. The fire
roared at the silent skies, a living spire
of human heat, continuing to smoulder
next morning in the amber autumn air…

And guys were ritualistically burnt
on bonfires up and down the land that night.
The human sacrifice can hit you hard:
the dead and dying lifted from the charred-
black wreckage of their bomb-shelter. The sight,
the memory, that says: no lessons learnt

again this year… The Gulf War *should* have taught
the Sainsbury Socialists a thing or two:
In modern war, a Patriot's a weapon.
A Tory is a creature you could step on.
An enemy's a friend you pander to –
as long as they have cash, we can be bought.

A century ago, they named the streets
they built in honour of the Whigs and Tories
who waged the Empire's wars; hence Ladysmiths
and Mafekings and Gladstone Streets. Such myths
seem callow now, naïve; and faded glories
are just as full of pathos as defeats.

And who today would ever think to name
a Thatcher Street, a Major Road ahead?
A Goose Green Mews, or a Kuwaiti Crescent?
A Baghdad Boulevard? No: in the present,
our glorious leaders (like our glorious dead)
aren't deemed to be deserving of such fame…

Once, Thatcher preached survival of the fitter
then closed the factories that the tool-setter
and fitter had maintained. So how could they
survive? How could they work and earn their pay?
(And how could she survey without regret a
proud people so impoverished and bitter?)

Now Thatcher's gone, stabbed with a friend's stiletto
when others thought they saw the vision clearer.
But in Fresh Fields the Left are still alive;
and, weaving dreams and dreadlocks, they survive
another year, another post-war era.
They soldier on. Long live the Muesli Ghetto!

1991

Thrift

I   Cadbury's

My parents' sole indulgence
was thrift.

There was no twist of string,
no mug of rusty nails,
that wouldn't 'come in'.

And food was better boiled,
lest we nurture a taste for flavours,
untempered riches.

She watered the mother's milk
in our drinking chocolate,
which was spooned into cups
with such ration-book restraint

as if to say:
we can't afford the laxity
of luxury.

II   Cox's

An apple a day…

No wives' tale, this,
but a warning:

sailors risked their lives
putting fruit in that bowl

and it's not for eating
– at least not all at once!

But I was with her when she bought them
from the greengrocer's.

What sailors?

The day I left –
a questioning stab at rebellion:

Bought two plump apples,
their skins waxed and rouged like women.

Ate both in a morning.

Nothing bad happened.

III   Cusson's

Care-worn shard,
thin sliver of fish
lies dying in the dish.

Take this slender minnow,
press it to the bulging keel,
the sheen of a broad new bar...

> *A ritual I must have learned early:*
> *wasting not, wanting not,*

... the taut scented skin at first unbending.
But in time, they merge:
softening hands work them in.

> *as she taught me,*
> *a practised denial polished through the years;*

In time, there's no dividing line,
no separate identities, just a child's hand,
pressed into a parent's, enclosed, enfolded...

> *so that something continues,*
> *here in the shard of my hand:*

> care-worn, a molecule has burrowed in,
> a spell, a glint from her first-ever gift to me

… a pregnancy, eccentric, a barrow-bulge,
a ley-line, discernible only
from the tilting wing of an escaping plane.

IV   Thrift

'It wasn't George "Dubya" Bush who said "carry on shopping" but Mayor Rudy Giuliani, addressing the citizens of New York City within hours of September 11 2001.' (The Guardian)

He knew a thing or two about late-state Capital.
He knew the twin spines of the economy
 – buying and selling –
would collapse in disarray
without a firm hand at the helm,
an encouraging word to the wise,
that judicious stitch in time.

She could have told him:
there is no tear in the fabric
that cannot be stitched back together
given patience, application,
and a bite of cotton, just the right length;

and above us, that attic,
silent with the weight of a trillion empty buttons,
random-single in dented tins
or threaded through the eye in DNA-strings,
all awaiting their moment;

and the ribbon-twists,
the mouse-nests of rubber bands,
the sparkle-silent jam-jars,
the cereal packets, snipped into squares
for messages and milkman-lists…

The day I left,
looking for a fight to cause for
(getting out
from under the breathless boxes of cloth,
the skeins of silent wool,
the glove-box teethed with needles),

and missing the point:
too busy on the blinkered barricades,
posing with paperback banners,
willfully penniless in a time of plenty,
thinking that merely not joining in
was enough to bring the tower down...

She could have told me
if I could have listened:
the most subversive thing we do
(we shivering minnows in the shark-market
that must keep moving to stay in business)
is refuse to buy so much.

The customary, post-war thrift of her,
constant all along,
as revolutions came and went;
as progress came, and went;
as flags and fashions and rubble-ruins
came and went;
as hippies, fellow-travellers, reds and greens
came and went.

She could have told us,
if only we'd stop spinning
long enough to listen:

Check the hem.

Make do.
Mend.

Darn.
(Reclaim the word.)

Knit together.
Get weaving.

Together,
we might just stall
the remorseless machine.

Cross Words

A flag of truce. An armistice. A pause…
It's hard to talk to dads: they've been in wars.
They're victims of their gender, or their era:
they're products of their dads – their pride, their fears,
their wordlessness… It's taken forty years
for me to find a way of getting nearer

to things he'd never bring himself to say.
(A man who shows his feelings is, well, gay.
It's just not done. You gauge another man
by how he throws a punch, or kicks a ball,
sinks pints or wins pub quizzes; physical
expressions… Keep your distance if you can,

and keep it cryptic, if your son should try
to ask about your feelings on the sly!)
It's puzzling… we have (one) a cross to bare…
We've never shared an angry word… Such puns
become the way for fathers and their sons
to talk in riddles of the thing they share:

We call a spade a playing card – of course.
A spanner is a bridge between two shores,
and honesty's a flower is a stream.
A legend is a foot, and time's a herb.
A lie's a lie; or maybe it's a verb,
and nothing's ever what it ought to seem.

So - meaning means that everything is hidden,
and anagrams occur to you unbidden,
and stories sound like other people's flaws…
Your brain's dog-legged, oblique, and in your eyes,
all words are just another in disguise,
and love… it's just a word for tennis scores.

Love's nothing: it's the 'o' in schizophrenia.
It's scattered through the Louvre. It's in Slovenia.

It's anagrammed, or turning, in revolver.
It's back there – at the start of evolution.
It's wrapped in gloves, dissolved in the solution
(for lover's just an anagram of solver!).

The chequered flag. It's there in black and white.
My dad would rather take his pen and write
the answer to 9 Down in 4 Across
than say he loved me. But I know it's there –
as sure as eggs have layers. So I care…
And as for being loved – he's at a loss:
he doesn't have a clue when love's in clover.
A learner-lover – that's my dad ALL OVER!

Vowel Play

I   Adam

A man may grab a hat and walk away
and stalk bazaars, black-starry Samarkand,
a calm Sahara caravan at bay…
A man may walk that far and fragrant land.

A man may grasp a hand that warms at last;
may watch - a hawk that scans a vacant dark.
A sad and angry flag may hang half-mast:
a man may fan that crazy fatal spark.

A man may act and gladly play a part;
may charm a party; spawn a bastard law;
may scrawl a chalk-mark wall, and call that Art;
a man may march at arms and start a war
(a Falklands War,
      a Balkan War,
            an Afghan War,
                    a Baghdad War…).

As Adam span, that vagrant, pagan day,
a man may want what's always cast astray:

that happy man shall fall at last and pray!

II   Eve

My eyes were kestrels. Hers were vervels, jesses.
Deep-red the sheen, her effervescent tresses.

The breezes blew her slender, temptress weeds.
The sweetest scent her gentle feet precedes.

Then be my sempstress, seel my tercel-eye!
Then tether me, let me desert the sky!

Enfetter me, my mew, my keep, my cell,
My Eve, my Everest… There's the even's knell!
Sweet helpmeet, wed me, 'ere the Vesper Bell!

III   Ingrid

I'm writing this film-script, this bright shiny thing:
slightly tight, slightly tipsy, six giggling girls
sit mingling, whilst jingling with glitzy-rich bling,
try singing (lip-synching) in shimmying swirls
whilst circling in giddily-dizzying twirls.

Slick Willy is sitting with Lizzy. Will's drinking,
imbibing still whisky in sly little sips.
'This spirit's insipid,' Will, glibly, is thinking
whilst wishing thin Lizzy will lick his thick lips.

Is this filly willing? Is this fishy nibbling?
(Lizzy is flirty, if shirtily shy…)
It's tricky. It's risky. Will's drippily dribbling
his spit in thin strings by his idling thigh.

Icily smiling, Will thinks Liz might kiss him,
might swim, skinny-dipping ('this bird's riding high!').
Silly Will isn't glimpsing: thin Lizzy will diss him,
dismiss him, if Ingrid slips sidling by.

In skimpy bikini, slim Ingrid's lip-biting,
this shy, virgin thing's blinking, flightily flirty;
whilst Lizzy is winking, is hinting, inviting
'Try lifting my skirt…' (which is mightily dirty!).

'Spilt milk!' Willy lisps, with his id limply shrinking.
'Girls frisky with girls,' Willy thinks, 'isn't right!
It's illicit, implicitly shittily-stinking!
I'll fight this indignity, try if I might!'

In grim cynicism, in crisis, Will's sinking,
whilst Ingrid is blind with this dim, misty sight:

Lizzy's wild, flinging kiss, gripping, vividly linking.
Timid Ingrid is simply limpid with light!

With this pithy skirmish, my film-script is finishing:
my writing is rhyming in ink which is dry.
In my sight, giddy misfits sit primly diminishing
whilst winningly grinning… My film critics sigh
with this stinging witticism: Pigs Might Fly!

IV   Gordon

Gordon Brown told Tony:
Don't hold on for too long,
for fools don't know how soon to go.
To stop's not strong; to go's not wrong,
so, sorry… Why so slow?!

Tony's words to Gordon:
Don't drool for my old job.
For good pontoon,
don't fold too soon.
Don't bow to crowd or mob.

Don't root for folly, Fools' Gold.
Don't cry for no sob-story.
Don't work from sorrow,
rob or borrow, now, tomorrow,
don't follow hollow glory.

So Gordon follows Tony:
top-job-dot-gov-dot-coms.
Soon doom looms down on London town:
horror drops two bombs.
Gordon stoops to look for
forty-two lost CD-ROMs.

Old-school crony donors,
from Commons or from Lords,
prod poor Gordon's voodoo doll
(only to follow protocol),
cross worthy Tory swords.

From Congo to Morocco,
from Oxford to Woodstock,
from Omsk or Tomsk, to Tokyo,
from Troon to Cork, or Knock,
worlds look down on Gordon,
on Gordon (Lost-Plot) Brown.

From Moscow to Toronto,
from Stockholm, Oslo, Bonn,
from top to bottom, root to blossom,
dot to polygon,
cold gods look down on Gordon,
(poxy oxy-moron),
on Gordon bloody Brown.

V   Gudrun

sultry sun stuns muggy UK suburbs

sky full – cumulus-tuft clumps
gulls buck – hug gusts
plump ducks flurry – scud – turn
surf's up – sub hulks rust un-sunk

trucks shunt slurry-muck
chuck up dust
rugby scrums churn muddy turf
surly punks skulk up gully-slums

fussy frumps cluck – tut
cuff runny-mucus runts
– shut-up!
push crumbly chunks up hungry gums

busy fun-pub – hurly-burly – rumpus
kung-fu thugs – rum-punch-drunk
munch spud-grub – slurp curry-mush
burp – trump – gulp sulphur-lungfuls
bully un-cuddly mutts
buy snuff – skunk – uncut smut

drug-ugly junky-mums – bulky-butch
thrust putty jug-full push-up D-cups
strut smug stuff
truss tucks up bulgy gut – but
lust just burns
blunt slugs uncurl – unfurl – pump up

hunky studs clutch gushy sluts
rub tummy – pluck rump – crush bust – strum crutch
clumsy hunch-buck humps
studs grunt – spurt musty suds

Gudrun sulks – sucks thumb
but stuck-up plummy yuppy guys
just shrug – sup bubbly – cut lunch – must run!
usury sucks up such lucky luxury

drums thud – cults tub-thump – gurus purr
fulcrums lurch – truth blurs – u-turns
untruth usurps truth – trust succumbs
dug-up skulls lurk dumbstruck by church

dusk-murmur – dull sputum sky
puny sun-blush lulls
mud-sunk – numbskull
fuddy-duddy – humdrum

dump

VI   Facetious

And when I pour ale in your accepting old cups… take it on trust.

All men, pious, abject, slipshod-drunk as they swig from full glasses: gin, port, rum… brazen it out.

Ascetics found abstemious ways best.

It's four a.m. Eight hours pass me in soft furls. Bra-less girls ovulate.

Slim boys – un-angelic on hurt-faded wings, ground-ascending through starless night-cloud, shaded in shroud-sad veils – slouch, arch evil, thought-flattering doubts; stand their ground and feint: 'On guard!' – fencing four-and-twenty iron-rusty blades.

In. Out.

Swaggering youths rage in chorus, fan the riot-hungry flames with cold fury. Hatred, involuntary evil, coughs. Angry tensions burst, dappled with shot pus.

And me? I'm – fortunately – inoculated. I'm so lucky!

Back then, I sought barren windows, hungry; gazed into rural regions: dull-scarlet hills, mould-shaped high mounds, blackening tough bracken; fibrous, glaze-icy ground attending my drought-slaked thirst.

Worst luck!

And then I'd pout, maybe… I would crave idols, uncanny, cretinous, scavenging souls, as tempting-young as pretty Miss-Worlds. Sluts!

And then I found charm: desirous and devious; facetious, and serious.

All envious.

An ending.

You.

Hinterland

Hinterland (noun), 1) a region lying inland from a port or centre of influence, 2) a place inhabited by people who only ever hint at things

My English teachers call them my False Friends:
between two languages are hinterlands
where tricks of mis-translation can be found.
A word can co-exist. A word can mean
two things at once. What looks like solid ground
is shifting, undermined. The word, in France,
for 'luck' is like the English word for 'chance'
- almost the same, but far enough away
to make a subtle difference between
the things we say and what we mean to say.

When I first came here (Was that luck? Or chance?)
I did not know the Rules: polite pretence,
the dance of diplomats, disguised, discreet…
There is a subtle diffidence between
the English and the foreigners they meet.
They say 'not bad', when what they mean is 'good'.
'You must' is said 'I kind of think you should'.
'I disagree' is said 'I couldn't say'.
'We must do this again' is pure smokescreen:
like 'See you soon', it means 'Please. Go away!'

You can't just call on friends; you have to phone
and make appointments. Everyone's alone,
behind locked doors, surrounded by belongings
(Reality's a giant plasma screen…)
and everyone's so laden with their longings,
the solid ground of houses could collapse.
(They'd blame the NUM round here, perhaps…)
And families subside. And fall apart.
Forgetfulness, of blood, and brain, and gene,
makes neighbours disregard their human heart.

My English teachers teach me 'sympathy'
- a word for fellow-feeling, empathy;
condolence, too, and pity... 'Sympathique',
that False French Friend, has meanings like congen-
ial, and likeable... My neighbours speak,
but only offer hints of understanding.
The search for 'sympathy' is never-ending
for foreigners like me. Confusion's rife,
and teachers don't explain what that will mean.
They only teach the language, not the life!

This Be Averse

They fuck you up, your girl and boy.
They don't intend to, but they do.
They ought to be your pride and joy,
but they will disillusion you.

For they've been disappointed by
their parents – you – who, they suspect,
arc fallible. You can't deny
that sense of dread, when you detect

they see through you. Familiar eyes
are mirrored there. You wonder whence,
from whom, they learned that cheap disguise:
rebellious indifference.

And so they spend their time on 'stuff',
so indolent it feels like crime,
forgetting you spent days enough
at their age, wasting precious time…

They take your life, your love, your looks,
your hopes, and every small advance,
and treat them like their own, the crooks,
without a single backward glance!

They sap your strength, they suck your blood,
they use your cash for things they buy,
and if it all runs as it should
your kids outlive you when you die.

And then they have the fucking nerve
to quote This Be The fucking Verse.
They get the parents they deserve -
or we, the kids (whichever's worse!).

Cryptic Diptych

I

When Simon read, a month or so ago,
the audience felt one of two reactions:
while most were entertained, and some impressed
(relieved it was accessible and funny,
admiring the self-deprecating wit,
the full-groan puns, the sad and knowing shrugs,
the slick delivery, bravery, bravura,
professional performance... not to mention
the clothes: all-black and effortlessly cool,
iconic - yet ironic - jeans and jacket),
there were a few who sneered, or sniffed disdain,
went home to air their doubts on web-site-blogs...

The problem was that Simon's poems rhyme
(admittedly a crime that's hard to bear).
But now – it's not reactionary, or twee
to write in rhyme. It's what the New Wave do!
Now rhyme is so passé, it's cool again,
a retro-chic rebellion on wings
iambic! And pentameters are just
the new blank verse! Perhaps we are aloof
and disapprove, we're envious-suspicious,
since rhyme is what 'best-selling' poets do...

Which leads us on to Simon's other crime:
his stuff is far too easily worked out,
there's not enough deciphering to do!
Some people like to work a little harder,
on poetry a little more oblique...
Then why succumb to snide Divide and Rule?
Instead of cherishing this thing we care

about, we get entrenched in haughty wars,
about if poems should or should not rhyme,
and should they be impenetrably cryptic!

II

Think back to Leftie-types we used to know
and drink with: 'neo-' 'proto-' 'pseudo-' factions
that bickered through the Eighties like depressed
divorcées haggling over spoons and money
and treating former bed-fellows like shit;
politicos and stern pedantic pugs,
convinced their take on Marx was truer, purer
and everybody else's was dissention.
We didn't see it as Divide and Rule…
We couldn't hear ourselves above the racket
of our own voices barking the refrain:
'The RCP are crypto-Fascist dogs!'

You could have substituted, at the time,
a dozen different acronyms in there:
the CPGB, WRP,
SWP, to name a (precious) few…
Self-righteous, self-important little men,
we didn't notice the important things,
those precious, not pedantic, things, like: trust
and being open-hearted are a proof
against small-mindedness and that pernicious
and pettifogging politics that grew

from greed and envy round about that time.
Being generous, giving benefit of doubt
went out of fashion in those years. Into
the vacuum marched the Thatcher intifada,
and we forgot, for fear of seeming weak,
of being over-taken for a fool,
what being human is, and how to share…

In Left(ish)ness, we had a common cause -
if only we'd remembered this in time.
And Poetry's another. Hence this diptych.

Everything that Lives

I played the Westbrook Blake
in the car on the way to work,

and as the singer sang:
'The fields of Cows by Willan's farm...'

a runaway cow stopped two lanes of traffic
before being herded up a lane between fields.

And as the singer sang:
'Bright as fire, spreading into azure Wings...'

A rainbow's perfect arc above me
touched either side of Ilkeston.

And as the singer sang:
'For everything that lives is Holy...'

I sat in the special-school car park
and a blonde-haired girl inside a taxi

pounded her angel-face
on the spittled window between us.

What's Left

For those of us who'd read *Das Kapital*,
who'd thought we were a stone's throw from Class War,
believed that History would prove us right
in time, in a millennium or two…
some twenty years have passed since we were left
illusion-less. The walls collapsed inside us,

as solid as the walls that fell around us.
We'd manned those barricades, fought Capital,
marched with the Miners, Laboured with the Left.
We'd kept the faith that won the last World War
from Fascism; and, somewhere in there, too,
the decent sense that Might's not always Right.

Despising the religions of the Right,
their God-AND-Mammon values (since for us
there was a Third Way to aspire to:
a human faith in human capital)…
Like photos of once-trendy clothes we wore,
that once-blind faith, that fashion, 's left

abandoned. And embarrassing. We're left,
two decades on, uncertain what was right
and what is Left… The media tut; make war
on Stalin, Mao, their purges… And for us
re-writing History is, to cap it all,
what gloating victors are entitled to…

We're losing our religion. Only to
emerge into a faithless age that's cleft
by two blind faiths: Consumer-Capital,
the 'shopping-is-my-fundamental-right'
of the corporate multinational U.S.;
and (so-called) Terror: Islam's 'Third World' War.

You need two gods to make a Holy War.
The daily ritual slaughter of these two

(both suicidal) tribes, anointing us
with oil and blood and sacrifice… We're left
inured and blinded, can't tell wrong from right,
we can't tell Whitehall from the Capitol…

It's tempting to forget that we're at war
when Capital makes sure The Price Is Right.
What's left, for those who used to think like us?

Fresh Fields Revisited

'You, who will emerge from the flood…'
(Bertolt Brecht)

I still see them around – or think I do:
those Radical Alternatives I slunk
around Fresh Fields with, back before the Flood:
all pipe-dream politics and well-chewed cud,
all Hope (all hopeless… good at getting drunk
but not much else…), all Discontent; all true
to principles we'd never quite thought through…
post-war, post-mod, post-hippy and post-punk;
post-Thatcher but pre-Blair: between the blood
of one war and the next, we felt that thud
of falling Wall, that crumbling concrete chunk
of History, those doomed certainties we knew.

The shift of dust on inner-city summers.
We moved on. Years, millennia, trod past.
The single mums got shacked up once again
(identical but different dodgy men);
the bijoux flats got rented out at last;
the post office got closed… And more newcomers,
new waves of Slovak wage-slaves, Polish plumbers
and Chinese cockle-pickers, in a fast-
incoming tide of willing workers, then
found harbour in our houses… which is when
the Left began to feel a tad mis-cast,
sad soldiers marching to last decade's drummers,

all out of step. We might have once enjoyed
that sense of dislocation, the romance
of acting like the Enemy Within,
the thrill of living in some different skin
and looking at this craven world askance,
through eyes half-cynical, half paranoid.
Not any more. We're overnight devoid
of ideology, denied our stance,

our voice, our vote (all politics akin
to PR now – mere marketing and spin…):
the Left-behind without a backward glance,
ignored, redundant, worse than unemployed!

Yet we survived, in spite of these reverses,
and found work, in this enterprising state.
There's no real industry here any more,
no manufacturing, machine-shop floor;
we don't make anything that's worth its weight,
that's more than virtual… And what is worse is
there's floods of work: for psychiatric nurses;
for arbitration lawyers at Relate;
for counsellors in drink, or drugs; or for
cash-management advisors to the poor;
for voices in the Homelessness debate;
for the Forces; for the men who drive the hearses…

We'd dreamed of being radical and free,
Alternative, such well-red renegades…
Free-Radicals, today, has come to mean
… some science-thing. And Alternative's now seen
as – not the actions of the Red Brigades –
but the in-word for some latest Therapy:
hope burns in ear-candles, or Feng-Shui,
not Molotovs, Kalashnikovs, grenades…
What's happened in the decades in between?
We switched, like traffic lights, from Red to Green.
We clambered off the burning barricades
and onto our allotments… These days, we

just cycle, and re-cycle, and compost,
with all the zeal of Stalin's later purges,
the fervour of the late Marquis de Sade.
The Stasi can't have kept a better guard
on the litter of our lives; on what emerges
from the land-fill; from the place where all is lost…
We fought the fight, and didn't count the cost,
to free Mankind from self-inflicted scourges…

Somehow the struggle never seemed so hard
as battling with the broccoli and chard…
Or so rewarding… Green organic verges
adorn this brave new world, this tempest-tossed

embattled little planet… But the prize,
the fight, the dream, might just be worth the candle,
this time, perhaps… and with a bit of luck,
this flood-plain place, half-doomed and half-dumbstruck,
half-starved, half-bloated, might just stop the scandal
of all those multinationals… Human eyes
have always looked for clear and cloudless skies…
I see them still, my old mates from The Randall…
And do we ever say 'Ey-up mi duck!'?
Or 'Do you ever hear from…?' Do we fuck!
We wouldn't want a scene we couldn't handle:
we're older, now, perhaps, but none too wise.

We'd rather act as if we'd never met,
embarrassed by that unremembered name.
No eyebrow raised, no tipping of the hat,
no kismet-karma, fate, or fancy-that;
no irony, or sense of it's-a-shame,
no rueful nod to mutual regret
for a past we've all been trying to forget…
We Keepers of a Long-Extinguished Flame
prefer it when we're not reminded that
we feel like we've been taken for a twat,
caught cheating at some complex life-like game,
or lost a fortune on some reckless bet…

At festivals, fresh fields of puddled mud:
on car-boot stalls, recycling Sunday junk;
or selling things: Lust, Envy, Supershoe;
or subway-sleeping under Waterloo;
in bars in Amsterdam, concussed on skunk;
on Crimewatch UK, up before m'lud;
or passed out on some pavement, caked in crud,
drunk mutton dressed as mutton, leaking spunk…
I see us – or I sometimes think I do.

The spectacle has never seemed so true:
A hopeful-hopeless generation shrunk
in the jetsam and the flotsam of the flood.

2008

The Digital Age in Middle Age

Now why did I come
all the way upstairs? Oh yes,
a memory-stick.

Notes

Some of these poems have previously been published in *Envoi*, Jo Bell (ed) *A Tale of Three Cities - New Writing from Derby, Leicester and Nottingham* (2006) and Andy Croft (ed) *Speaking English - Poems for John Lucas* (2007). Thanks are due to the editors and publishers concerned.

Thrift
A spell is also a dialect word for a splinter.

Adam
I am indebted to a former brother-in-law, who long ago supplied the first line.

Eve
Vervels and jesses are falconry terms for the ties that secure birds of prey. Tercel and tercelgentle are words for a hawk. To seel is the practice of sewing up the eyelids of a hawk, to subdue and control it.

Facetious
There are only two English words in which all five vowels appear in alphabetical order. They are both in this poem.

Hinterland
Thanks to Khaldoun Alhindi for supplying the final line, and more, to this poem.

Everything that Lives
Bright as Fire is a CD of settings of William Blake by Mike Westbrook.

Fresh Fields Revisited
'The Spectacle is a permanent opium war which aims to make people identify consumer goods with commodities and satisfaction with survival... From the automobile to television, all the goods selected by the Spectacular system are also its weapons for a constant reinforcement of the conditions of isolation, of "lonely crowds." Guy Debord, *Society of the Spectacle*.